TRAIL OF TEARS

Trail of

Tears

By Sue Vander Hook

Content Consultant
Rowena McClinton
Associate Professor, Department of Historical Studies
Southern Illinois University, Edwardsville

ABDO
Publishing Company

CREDITS

Published by ABDO Publishing Company, 8000 West 78th Street,
Edina, Minnesota 55439. Copyright © 2010 by Abdo Consulting
Group, Inc. International copyrights reserved in all countries. No
part of this book may be reproduced in any form without written
permission from the publisher. The Essential Library™ is a
trademark and logo of ABDO Publishing Company.

Printed in the United States of America,
North Mankato, Minnesota
092009
012010

 PRINTED ON RECYCLED PAPER

Editor: Paula Lewis
Copy Editor: Erika Wittekind
Interior Design and Production: Emily Love
Cover Design: Emily Love

Library of Congress Cataloging-in-Publication Data
Vander Hook, Sue, 1949-
  Trail of Tears / Sue Vander Hook.
     p. cm. — (Essential events)
  ISBN 978-1-60453-946-2
  1. Trail of Tears, 1838-1839—Juvenile literature. 2. Cherokee
Indians—Relocation—Juvenile literature. 3. Cherokee Indians—
History—Juvenile literature. [1. Indians of North America—
Southern States—History.] I. Title.
  E99.C5V36 2010
  975.004'97557—dc22
                                    2009031066

TABLE OF CONTENTS

The Cherokee Trail of Tears memorial overlooks the Arkansas River.

NUNNA DUAL TSUNY

The Cherokee call the "trail where we cried" the *Nunna dual Tsuny*. But the Trail of Tears, as it came to be known, was more than a trail. It was the forced exile and removal of the Cherokee from their homeland in America's Deep South. It was the darkest hour for one of America's native tribes and is a controversial aspect in the history of the United States. The Cherokee were not the only American Indians to be displaced. The Choctaw, the Seminole, the Creek, the Chickasaw, and others also had to leave the lands of their ancestors.

FORCED TO LEAVE

Prior to 1830, some American Indians voluntarily left their homelands and headed west. But from 1831 to 1839, thousands of American Indians, including the Cherokee, were forced from their land east of the Mississippi River. In 1830, U.S. Congress passed and President Andrew Jackson signed the Indian Removal Act into law. This act ordered the removal of American Indians in the Southeast. The U.S. government set aside an area known as Indian Territory for the relocation of American Indians. The troops were carrying out orders from the president of the United States.

In 1838, as many as 17,000 Cherokee were forced to leave their ancestral land. The first group of approximately 3,000 left in June during an extremely brutal summer of heat and drought. Some were packed into two-story flatboats and transported on the Tennessee, Ohio, Mississippi, and Arkansas rivers. Those who left in the fall walked most of the way. Some took a southern route through lower Tennessee and across Arkansas. Others headed north through western Kentucky, the southern tip of Illinois, and Missouri. Still others followed paths in the middle. But they all ended up in western Arkansas and eastern Oklahoma.

George Hicks, one of the Cherokee leaders, left with a group in November.

A Personal Account

From 1773 to 1776, more than 60 years before the Trail of Tears, American naturalist William Bartram explored eight southern colonies. He traveled through Indian country and observed the Seminole, the Creek, and the Cherokee. In the late 1780s, he wrote about his journeys. His writings are considered an accurate account of the events and native peoples of America. He described the Cherokee as:

tall, erect, and moderately robust, their limbs well shaped, so as generally to form a perfect human figure; their features regular, and [face] open, dignified, and placid; yet the forehead and brow so formed as to strike you instantly with heroism and bravery; the eye, though rather small, yet active and full of fire; the iris always black, and the nose commonly inclining [like an eagle's beak].

Their complexion of a reddish brown or copper colour; their hair, long, lank, coarse, and black as a raven.

The women of the Cherokee are tall, slender, erect and of a delicate frame—their features formed with perfect symmetry; their [faces] cheerful and friendly; and they move with a becoming grace and dignity.[1]

On November 4, 1838, he wrote with sadness:

> *We are now about to take our leave and kind farewell to our native land, the country that the great spirit gave our Fathers . . . it is with sorrow that we are forced by the authority of the white man to [leave] the scenes of our childhood . . . we bid a final farewell to it and all we hold dear.* [2]

The Cherokee who left their land that fall battled rain, sleet, snow, ice, and extreme cold on their three-month journey. The aged and the sick rode in government-supplied wagons, and a few people rode on horseback. But the majority walked, clad with inadequate shoes and clothing that offered little protection from the harsh elements.

The removal of the Cherokee cost thousands of lives—thousands who were removed from their homeland and never made it to their new land. Some died from disease and starvation in the stockades where they were kept prisoners before the journey began. Others lost their lives

"My friends, circumstances render it impossible that you can flourish in the midst of a civilized community. You have but one remedy within your reach, and that is to remove to the west. And the sooner you do this, the sooner you will commence your career of improvement and prosperity." [3]

—Andrew Jackson, addressing Cherokee leaders, 1835

Cherokee Nation

The Cherokee Nation is recognized by the U.S. government as a sovereign nation, whose independent status was granted by treaty and by law. In 1901, Congress gave U.S. citizenship to all American Indians residing in Indian Territory.

On September 5, 1975, the constitution of the Cherokee Nation was approved by the Commissioner of Indian Affairs. It was ratified by the Cherokee people on June 26, 1976.

on the long, difficult journey. They died on the crowded, disease-infested flatboats or from exhaustion on the trails. Family members stopped along the trail just long enough to bury their dead in shallow graves, and then they moved on.

Approximately 4,000 Cherokee died on the Trail of Tears. The exiles who survived settled near Tahlequah, Oklahoma, and founded the Cherokee Nation. Today, their descendents make up the largest American Indian tribe in the United States, with more than 250,000 members. Another group of Oklahoma Cherokee formed the United Keetoowah Band of Cherokee Indians. It has approximately 10,000 members today.

Not all the Cherokee ended up in Oklahoma. Those who had negotiated the Treaty of 1819 forfeited their rights to the lands of the Cherokee Nation. Their chief,

John Ross, asked Congress to protect them from removal. They grew to be a tribe of approximately 10,000 and became the Eastern Band of the Cherokee Nation.

AN ETERNAL FLAME

In 1984, almost 150 years after the Trail of Tears, members of the Cherokee Nation and the Eastern Band of Cherokee met at Red Clay, Tennessee. It was the first time members of the tribes had been together since their ancestors were separated in 1838. The two groups lit an eternal flame, and Cherokee runners carried the torch 150 miles (241 km) through the mountains before placing it at Red Clay. It was the beginning of regular meetings between the two tribes.

In 1989, members of the two tribes met in Cherokee, North Carolina, to commemorate the 150th anniversary of the Trail of Tears. Wilma Mankiller, chief of the Cherokee Nation at the time, attended the anniversary. Later she wrote:

> Although it is so crucial for us to focus on the good things—our tenacity, our language and culture, the revitalization of tribal communities—it is also

A Woman Chief

Wilma Mankiller was the first woman to serve as principal chief of the Cherokee Nation. She served from 1985 to 1995. While she was chief, the Cherokee Nation doubled its membership as well as its tribal budget. She supervised programs that helped teens acquire job skills and provided economic aid for industries and businesses in the Cherokee Nation. In 1991, she stated, "Given our history of adversity I think it's a testament to our tenacity, both individually and collectively as a people, that we've been able to keep the Cherokee Nation government going since time immemorial."[5]

In 1998, President Bill Clinton awarded her the Presidential Medal of Freedom, the highest award given to an individual who has made an exceptional contribution to the United States.

important that we never forget what happened to our people on the Trail of Tears. It was indeed our holocaust.[4]

The removal of thousands of American Indians from their homeland changed a people and altered a nation forever. That tragic chapter is imprinted in U.S. history and in the hearts of the Cherokee.

Wilma Mankiller received a Presidential Medal of Freedom from President Clinton in January 1998.

Chapter 2

American Indian village in the Virginia colony in the 1600s

WEST IS BLACK,
BLACK IS DEATH

The emotional and physical scars of forced migration ran deep for the American Indians—especially for the Cherokee. They suffered greatly due to the loss of lives. It also brought an end to the legacy of their ancestral lands.

In Balance with Nature

For centuries, Cherokee women had farmed the land. Cherokee men had fished and hunted to provide food and clothing for their families. But they were careful to take from nature only what they needed. According to their beliefs, the Cherokee participated in seven religious ceremonies per year to remain in balance with nature. The ceremonies celebrated the new growing season, the first ears of corn, the first moon of fall, and more.

The earth with its rich soil, plants, animals, mountains, and rivers was also a part of the Cherokees' spiritual life. They believed the gods were in the mountains, in the sun, and in fire. Objects of nature—such as rocks, animals, birds, rivers, and trees—took on human names and characteristics. The Cherokee believed in Long Man the River, a caring being whose water cleansed a person of illness and sin. *Dayunisi*, the water beetle, brought up mud and formed the earth. The Great Buzzard sculpted the Great Smoky Mountains with its wings. The Raven Mocker was the most dreaded spirit. Its shrieking heralded the imminent death of a Cherokee.

The Cherokee believed that each direction held particular significance. North was blue and symbolized trouble and defeat. South was white and brought peace and happiness. East, the way of light and sun, was red and led to success. But west led to the Darkening Land, and it was black for death. When the Cherokee were forced to migrate west, they headed in the direction they despised and feared.

ARRIVAL OF THE WHITE MAN

The Cherokee had lived in North America longer than anyone knew. They lived on land in present-day Georgia, Tennessee, North Carolina, South Carolina, and parts of West Virginia, Kentucky, and Alabama. Much of their land was in the rugged Appalachian Mountains. Other tribes—the Creek, the Choctaw, the Chickasaw, and the Seminole—also had established their societies in the Southeast. Sometimes, the tribes were at war with each other for land, dominance, and individual honor as warriors.

American Indians had rich, colorful cultures, languages, and traditions. However, their way of

Origin

A variety of theories speculate about where the Cherokee and other tribes originated and when they first came to North America. Some say that American Indians came from Asia into present-day Alaska by way of a land bridge that formed in the Bering Strait during the last ice age. It is said that they followed the direction of the sunrise to a warmer climate in North America. As they settled in different areas, they cultivated their own languages and cultures.

The de Soto expedition discovered the Mississippi River in 1540 and encountered American Indians.

life was interrupted with the arrival of European explorers, who called them Indians. The first known Europeans to have contact with the Cherokee were members of Hernando de Soto's Spanish expedition. In 1540, the Cherokee may have met white men searching for gold in present-day North Carolina. Their first encounter was friendly. The Cherokee shared corn and other food items with their visitors and played dice with them. But de Soto's men had been known to steal from other Indians and force some into slavery.

Other than Juan Pardo's Spanish expedition of 1566 to 1568, more than a century would pass before there were any further records of Cherokee encounters with Europeans. In the late 1600s, English and French traders sought out the Cherokee for their furs and deerskins. In exchange, the Cherokee received iron and steel tools, brass kettles, hoes, knives, guns, ammunition, and

Cherokee Culture

Women were an important part of Cherokee society. Daughters inherited houses and land from their mothers. Cherokee women had political power as leaders and warriors. Family history was traced through the mother. Children belonged to the mother's clan. The Cherokee culture has seven clans with specific characteristics:

- Wolf Clan: The largest and only clan allowed to kill wolves; usually the war chief is from this clan
- Deer Clan: Keepers of the deer, fast runners, and good hunters
- Long Hair Clan: Wear their hair in a unique way; usually the peace chief is from this clan
- Bird Clan: Keepers of the birds
- Wild Potato Clan: Keepers of the land
- Blue Clan: Makes medicine for children
- Paint Clan: Medicine people

As clan affiliations are not documented in a written form, most Cherokee today do not know their clan affiliation.

The Cherokee language has a musical quality and a precise rhythm. Approximately 10 percent of the Cherokee population still speaks the Cherokee language. The Cherokee perpetuate their culture by continuing to use their language. Some aspects of their culture can only be expressed in their native language as there are no equivalent words in English.

trinkets. The Europeans also supplied the Cherokee with rum and whiskey, which created disorder within the tribe. Some English traders became part of the Cherokee communities by marrying Indian women and establishing families.

For the most part, the explorers were friendly. But a new unseen enemy lurked among the Cherokee that they could not defeat. The Europeans brought diseases with them that American Indians were not immune to. The first documented epidemic of smallpox occurred in 1698. For years, smallpox and measles struck North American tribes. By the early 1700s, approximately 50 percent of the Cherokee population had died from diseases introduced by Europeans. The Cherokee population dwindled to approximately 20,000 people.

Alliances and Wars

European contact with the Cherokee became more frequent. France, Spain, and England competed for control of North American land and for alliances with Indian tribes. In 1730, the Cherokee allied with England. A group of seven Cherokee chiefs traveled to London to meet with King George II and finalize a treaty. The chiefs

The Flag of a Nation

At the center of the current Cherokee Nation flag is the Great Seal of the Cherokee Nation. In the center of the seal is a seven-pointed star, which represents the seven Cherokee clans. Around the seal are seven yellow stars, each with seven points, which also symbolize the tribal clans. In 1989, a seven-pointed black star was added to the upper right corner of the flag. The large black star represents the light that went out with the deaths of those who died on the Trail of Tears.

returned with a treaty that promised England's protection of Cherokee land. It also committed the Cherokee to fight for England.

By 1754, France and England were at war over land in North America. The French and Indian War (1754–1763) forced American Indians to take sides, and most sided with France. But the British, who had the Cherokee as allies, were victorious. However, Virginia settlers slaughtered 24 Cherokee warriors. Cherokee retaliated by attacking settlers in Virginia and North Carolina. The governor of South Carolina declared war on the Cherokee. Indian homes and towns were burned. The Cherokee lost much of their land and retreated to the mountains. Their conflicts with the colonists were not over, however. In 12 years, they would find themselves embroiled in the American Revolution.

King George II of England

*The British made alliances with the Indians
during the American Revolution.*

THIS LAND IS OUR LAND

In 1775, American colonists revolted against England. The American Revolution had begun. The Cherokee soon became soldiers as well as victims of the war. They paid a dear price for their British alliance.

Colonists burned down more than 50 Cherokee cities, slaughtered their horses and cattle, and burned their crops. They brutalized Cherokee warriors. They killed and scalped Cherokee women. The death toll was high, and the war devastated Cherokee land. Most Cherokee surrendered to the colonists by 1781.

The colonists won the long, bloody, eight-year war. They gained their independence from Britain as well as control of the 13 colonies. Within those borders was land that belonged to American Indians.

Taking Land from the Tribes

The new independent nation created the Articles of Confederation and a Confederation Congress that governed the young nation until 1789. Because the Indians had primarily allied with the British, they were treated as conquered nations. This allowed the states to feel justified in confiscating land of the Cherokees.

Land belonging to other tribes was also taken away. Although the Cherokee and other southern tribes wanted a peaceful solution, northern tribes reacted violently. Warfare broke out in several areas of the country. In an effort to end the fighting, the U.S. government encouraged the individual tribes to sign peace treaties.

Treaties, Negotiations, and Plans

On November 28, 1785, the Cherokee signed the Treaty of Hopewell. It was designed to bring peace between the United States and the Cherokee. The treaty defined new Cherokee boundaries and gave the tribe authority to get rid of unwanted white settlers. The treaty was signed by 4 representatives of the United States and 37 leaders and warriors of the Cherokee tribe. However, it was not honored by the individual states.

Support for the King

During the American Revolution, colonists encouraged American Indians to remain neutral. But most American Indians supported Great Britain and King George III. They viewed the colonies' struggle for independence also as a struggle for Indian land. The Iroquois Confederacy had 1,500 men who fought for the British. Joseph Brant, a member of the Mohawk tribe and an officer in the British army, became infamous for his raids on colonial settlements in New York and Pennsylvania.

In July 1776, Brant worked with British General William Howe to take New York from the colonists. He also traveled to Indian villages to convince members of the tribes to join the British. In July 1777, four nations of the Iroquois Confederacy of the Six Nations (Seneca, Cayuga, Onondaga, and Mohawk throughout central New York) decided to enter the war on the side of the British. The Tuscarora and Oneida nations supported the Americans. When colonial forces secured New York in 1779, Indians loyal to the king were forced into Canada. Joseph Brant died on November 24, 1807.

North Carolina and Georgia believed that the states, not the federal government, had authority over the land. They continued to expand onto Indian land. In January 1786, the Choctaw and Chickasaw tribes entered into their own Hopewell Treaties that also set new boundaries for their lands.

It was a challenge for the newly formed United States to determine how its citizens would live among American Indians. When the U.S. Constitution was formed in 1787, it gave Congress and the president authority over Indian affairs and trade. President George Washington gave the task of dealing with the Indians to Henry Knox, the first secretary of war.

Within a few months, Knox laid out a plan to stop the fighting and protect the Indian tribes as sovereign, independent nations. He called the intrusion of settlers onto Indian land disgraceful. But it was nearly impossible to remove the thousands of settlers who had already encroached on land that did not belong to them. So Knox negotiated with the

Treaty of Paris

The Treaty of Paris, signed on September 3, 1783, officially ended the American Revolution. The last British soldiers left American soil on November 25, 1783. Great Britain agreed to the Treaty of Paris without consulting its Indian allies. The treaty gave the land between the Appalachian Mountains and the Mississippi River, which rightfully belonged to the American Indians, to the United States.

Henry Knox

Henry Knox, the first U.S. secretary of war, was a bookseller in Boston, Massachusetts, before the American Revolution. He served as chief artillery officer in the Continental army during the war. General George Washington was impressed with Knox and made him a colonel and later a major general.

As secretary of war, Knox was responsible for managing U.S. relations with American Indians. He supported the Trade and Intercourse Acts, which set up the U.S. "civilization" program in 1790. He also encouraged the new government to honor its treaties with the American Indians. However, time and again, the United States allowed settlers to pour into land protected by the treaties. Knox left his government position in 1795 and settled on an estate in Thomaston, Maine. Fort Knox in Kentucky, Fort Knox in Maine, and Knoxville, Tennessee, are all named in his honor.

Cherokee: the United States would pay Indians for the land that had been taken away and forbid further intrusion on tribal land.

Knox also acknowledged that when "civilized" and "uncivilized" people try to live together, the "uncivilized" usually do not survive. He believed that if the Indians were to live on, they would have to become a "civilized" people. At that time, this meant living like white Americans with roots in European culture. Knox set out to integrate Indians into American society.

President Washington's cabinet members, left to right, *Henry Knox, Thomas Jefferson, Alexander Hamilton, and Edmund Randolph*

Indians bartered furs for goods at trading posts.

A Greater Degree
of Civilization

lthough the Cherokee had been farming for centuries, their active involvement in the fur trade led the U.S. government to believe they were hunters who lived only on wild food. The conditions for "civilizing" the Cherokee were specified in the 1791 Treaty of Holston. It stated in part:

> *That the Cherokee nation may be led to a greater degree of civilization, and to become herdsman and cultivators, instead of remaining in a state of hunters, the United States will from time to time furnish . . . useful implements of [farming] and further assist the said nation.*[1]

The U.S. government delivered hoes, plows, axes, spinning wheels, and cottonseeds to the people they considered hunter-gatherers. It appointed people to live among the Cherokee and teach them "civilized" ways. Experienced blacksmiths, millers, and spinners taught the Cherokee new skills. The Indians learned how to grow cotton and raise sheep.

The Cherokee were willing learners who realized they must adapt to survive. They learned quickly, and many prospered and became wealthy. Some owned plantations and even purchased African-American slaves to work in their fields. Others operated ferries or established taverns and stores. Cherokee women learned to spin cotton and wool and weave it into beautiful cloth that sold for a high price.

Efforts by the U.S. government to "civilize" the Cherokee were succeeding, but its motives were not always pure. The government wanted more Indian land. It repeatedly negotiated new treaties with the Cherokee—treaties that redefined land borders and gave more territory to the United States.

The government also operated trading posts on Cherokee land. The Cherokee could purchase equipment and supplies there, as well as goods such as coffee and sugar. White Americans freely extended credit to Indians. And when the Indians could not pay back their debts, whites readily accepted land as payment.

A New President and New Deals

When Thomas Jefferson became the third president of the United States in 1801, he continued the "civilization" plan created by George Washington and Henry Knox. Jefferson, too, wanted to be on friendly terms with the tribes and "civilize" them.

But most of all, he wanted more of their land. The Trade and Intercourse Act of 1802 gave the president the authority to "promote civilization among the friendly Indian tribes, and . . . to cause them to be furnished with useful domestic animals, and implements of [farming]."[2] Jefferson hoped the Indians would become farmers and give up

The United States in 1803 after the Louisiana Purchase

hunting, which would free up hunting grounds for white settlers. But Jefferson was disappointed in the amount of land the Indians were willing to sell.

Jefferson made a deal with the state of Georgia. In the Compact of 1802, he promised to eliminate Cherokee land titles in Georgia and remove the Cherokee from the state. By Jefferson's second term, he broadened his goals to relocate every tribe east of the Mississippi River. He called Indians "noble savages" who could not exist in a growing United

States. The Louisiana Purchase of
1803 gave Jefferson a place where the
tribes could be relocated. He believed
Indians could live more peacefully
west of the Mississippi River, free
from the intrusion of white American
settlers.

A Culture Undergoing Changes

However, the Indian tribes
were changing and adapting to
European-American culture. They
altered aspects of their traditions and
religions. For example, in 1800, the
Cherokee allowed Moravians to open
a mission. At first, the Cherokee
made it clear they did not want a
new religion. They readily accepted
the missionaries' offer to establish
schools, but it would be nine years
before the Cherokee would accept
Christianity. When Second Principal
Chief Charles Hicks converted to
Christianity, few Cherokee followed
his example.

Moving Westward

In 1803, the United
States purchased 827,987
square miles (2.14 mil-
lion sq km) of land from
France for $15 million.
The Louisiana Purchase,
as it was called, stretched
from the Mississippi River
to the Rocky Mountains,
doubling the size of the
United States. Settlers
moving west often en-
countered brutal conflicts
with American Indians
protecting their lands. The
United States designated
part of the land as Indian
Territory for relocation of
Indian tribes.

After the War of 1812, which ended in 1815, more missionary groups brought the Bible and Christian beliefs to the Cherokee. Many members of the tribe converted. They left behind their cultural religious traditions that linked nature with gods found in the mountains, sun, and fire.

Pleased that missionaries were "civilizing" the tribes, Congress funded their efforts. Missionaries brought religion, education, farming methods, and medicine to the tribes.

Written Laws and an Elected Leader

In 1821, a Cherokee named Sequoyah developed a written version of the Cherokee language. He created a symbol for each Cherokee sound—a syllabary or alphabet. Until that time, the Cherokee language was only spoken. Storytellers passed along traditions and tribal history from one generation to the next. The Cherokee memorized Sequoyah's 85 symbols and learned how to read and write in their own language. Some also became literate in English. In 1828, seven years after Sequoyah developed the Cherokee syllabary, Elias Boudinot published the first Indian newspaper, the *Cherokee Phoenix*. It was printed in Cherokee and English.

The Cherokee sought to modify their government and laws to reflect the U.S. legal system. This would sustain them as a legally recognized government among Americans. Written laws were established to prevent crime, protect property, and preserve the tribe. In 1827, the Cherokee developed their own constitution. It was modeled after the U.S. Constitution with executive, legislative, and judicial branches of government. The document defined Cherokee land boundaries and made it clear that individuals could not sell land. If tribal members

A Written Language

In 1821, a Cherokee silversmith named Sequoyah stood before members of his tribe and told them that he had found a way to write the Cherokee language. He showed them pieces of paper filled with 85 symbols that represented syllables in the Cherokee language.

He then asked his daughter Ahyoka to read the words. To prove that the symbols represented the Cherokee language, Sequoyah walked away from the crowd. While he was gone, the people told Ahyoka what to write down. When Sequoyah returned, he read aloud from Ahyoka's paper—exactly the words she had been told to write down. Sequoyah then offered more proof. Ahyoka left, and the crowd told Sequoyah what to write. When Ahyoka came back, she was able to read what the people had told her father to write down.

The Cherokee were convinced Sequoyah had, indeed, developed a written Cherokee language. Within one year, most Cherokee were able to read and write in their own language. In 1825, a translation of the New Testament was handwritten into the Cherokee language. In 1827, the Cherokee developed a written constitution.

moved to the West, they were stripped of their Cherokee citizenship.

In 1828, John Ross was elected principal chief of the Cherokee. His office and the center of Cherokee government were in New Echota, Georgia. Under Ross's leadership, Cherokee government and education continued to grow, and the people became more literate.

The Demand for More Land

The United States was also developing and growing. The number of U.S. citizens nearly doubled over a period of 20 years. By 1830, the United States had 24 states and almost 13 million people. The demand for land increased, and the tribes were pressured more and more to make room for white settlers.

For many years, the U.S. government had tried to convince all southeastern tribes to voluntarily relocate west of the Mississippi River.

John Ross

In 1817, John Ross was elected to the national Cherokee Council. From 1819 to 1826, he was the president of the council and helped write the Cherokee Constitution. In 1828, he became principal chief of the Cherokee until his death in 1866. Ross was only one-eighth Cherokee by blood. Although his wife, Quatie, had a stronger Cherokee lineage, she also was a mixed-blood Cherokee.

Some had migrated voluntarily, but most Indians, especially the Cherokee, refused to give up their homelands. A new U.S. president and the discovery of gold in Georgia—on Cherokee territory—would soon make relocation mandatory. The tribes would be forced to leave their land. ⌐

Sequoya with the Cherokee syllabary

Andrew Jackson

GOLD!

n 1827, Georgia legislators had proclaimed, "The lands in question belong to Georgia. She *must* and she *will* have them."[1] That year, Georgia successfully removed most Creek Indians from the state.

But Georgia was impatient with the federal government's failure to expel the Cherokee. By 1828, most Southerners supported Andrew Jackson in the presidential election. They believed he would remove the Indians from the South—a goal they had sought for nearly 30 years.

Jackson won the election handily, and Georgia confidently took more control of the Indian situation. In December, the Georgia legislature passed laws that stripped the Cherokee of most of their rights. State leaders hoped the restrictions would encourage the Cherokee to leave.

In 1829, Principal Chief John Ross took a delegation to address Congress in Washington DC. Ross claimed that Georgia's laws violated treaties between the Cherokee and the United States. Although Ross had the support of some senators, President Jackson said he would support Georgia. He claimed that the state had the right to enact laws that affected the Cherokee.

In Support of Indian Rights

In truth, Jackson's plan was to remove all Indians from every state. Some people, especially those from northern states, were outraged that tribes might be

Representative David Crockett

In 1827, at the age of 41, "Davy" Crockett was elected to represent the twelfth district of Tennessee in the U.S. House of Representatives. In 1831, he lost his bid for reelection. This was largely due to his opposition to President Andrew Jackson's Indian Removal Act. Crockett ran again and won in 1833 but was defeated twice for reelection in following years.

He left politics and went to Texas. He fought and died on March 6, 1836, in the Battle of the Alamo against the Mexican army.

His oldest son, John Wesley Crockett, later served in the House of Representatives for four years. He represented the same Tennessee district that his father had once represented.

forcefully removed from their land. Outspoken southern Congressman David "Davy" Crockett of Tennessee supported Indian rights and spoke against Jackson's plan.

Crockett and other opponents of Jackson's idea claimed that the Cherokee were "civilized" and ready to integrate into American life. Cherokee men and women dressed in European-style clothing. They were successful farmers, cattle ranchers, and business owners. Sequoyah's development of the Cherokee alphabet had led to rising literacy. The Cherokee had modern schools, churches, and roads. They also had a constitution with a representational form of government.

GOLD FEVER

Irate citizens signed petitions and published articles objecting to taking the Indians' land and exiling them to the West. But Jackson's backing was

Congressman David "Davy" Crockett

strong. The discovery of gold in northern Georgia made many determined to rid their state of Indians. Most of the gold ran through Cherokee land. This did not bode well for the Cherokee.

In 1829, thousands of miners in search of riches converged in the Southeast. Hoards of prospectors, called Twenty-Niners, set up camps. They dug for gold, indifferent to who owned the land. Boomtowns were built and provided food, lodging, and entertainment. Tension mounted between the miners and the Cherokee, who sometimes resorted to violence in order to protect their property. Greatly outnumbered, the Cherokee were defeated by the thousands of white miners in the Southeast. Prospectors also eyed the Cherokee's rich pastureland with cattle and sheep. They wanted the Indians' crops of corn, cotton, and potatoes.

Benjamin Parks, one of the first to find gold in Georgia, described the madness of the gold rush:

> *The news got abroad, and such excitement you never saw. It seemed within a few days as if the whole earth must have heard of [the gold]. . . . They came afoot, on horseback and in wagons, acting more like crazy men than anything else.*[2]

Gold fever was unstoppable. On December 19, 1829, the governor of Georgia announced that all Cherokee land, including gold mines, belonged to the state.

THE INDIAN REMOVAL ACT

A new bill was introduced in Congress. The Indian Removal Act (1830) was designed to rid all states of Indians. John Forsyth, former governor of Georgia, addressed Congress in support of the bill. He said that his state should never have to "submit to the intrusive sovereignty of a petty tribe of Indians." He called the Indians a "useless and burdensome" people and a "race not admitted to be equal."[3]

Others passionately defended the rights of the Indians. Vermont Senator Edward Everett addressed the Speaker of the House, "The evil, Sir, is enormous; the inevitable suffering incalculable. Do not stain the fair name of the country."[4]

After months of heated debate, Congress passed the Indian Removal Act by a narrow margin. President Jackson signed it into law on May 28, 1830. The new law allowed Jackson

Women and Human Rights

In 1829, American women became involved in the controversy over the Indian Removal Act. Although women could not vote or hold political office at that time, they were often involved in charitable and religious endeavors. Women had been major contributors to American Indian missions and considered the government's recent treatment of the Indians immoral. Prominent writer and educator Catherine Beecher took action and called on women to petition Congress not to pass the Indian Removal Act.

The women of America rallied and flooded Congress with hundreds of petitions and hundreds of thousands of signatures. Although Congress passed the act, the women's movement continued to speak up for and demand human rights.

to give unsettled land west of the Mississippi River to Indians in exchange for their land within the borders of existing states. Georgia prohibited Indians from mining gold or from meeting for political purposes, unless they wanted to sell their land. They also could not testify in court against a white person. In response, the Cherokee made it punishable by death for a Cherokee to sell land to white people.

Jackson sought to remove Indians from the states of Georgia, Tennessee, Alabama, Mississippi, and North Carolina. On December 6, 1830, Jackson justified his plan to Congress:

The removal of the Indians beyond the white settlements is approaching to a

Help from the Cherokee

General Andrew Jackson and the Cherokee were allies in the 1814 Battle of Horseshoe Bend. The intent of this battle was to clear the Red Stick Creek Indians out of Alabama to make way for U.S. settlements. Jackson probably would not have won the battle or survived without Cherokee help.

According to Cherokee oral history, a Creek Indian warrior was about to kill Jackson. However, Cherokee Chief Junaluska put a tomahawk through the Creek's skull, saving Jackson's life.

Jackson praised the Cherokee people and said, "You have shown yourselves worthy of the friendship of your Father the President of the United States—in battle you have been brave—in friendship steadfast."[5]

When Jackson signed the Indian Removal Act in 1830, the Cherokee felt betrayed by Jackson. They had considered him their friend.

happy consummation. . . . The consequences of a speedy removal will be important to the United States, to individual States, and to the Indians themselves. . . . It will place a dense and civilized population in large tracts of country now occupied by a few savage hunters.[6]

He added that clearing Alabama and Mississippi of their Indian populations would "enable those States to advance rapidly in population, wealth, and power."[7]

Jackson and the governor of Georgia hoped more Cherokee would move without force. According to an earlier treaty in 1828, the government would give "a good Rifle, a Blanket, and Kettle, and five pounds of Tobacco" to the head of any family who voluntarily enrolled for emigration.[8] Each family member would also get a blanket and receive support for one year and payment for personal belongings they left behind. A bonus of $50 was offered to anyone who took four other Cherokee with

Opposition

In 1829 and 1830, Jeremiah Evarts of Massachusetts released a series of letters to the press under the pseudonym William Penn. His letters were published in the Washington *National Intelligencer* and reprinted in the newspaper *Cherokee Phoenix*.

He opposed the forced removal of the Cherokee and seemed to suggest all-out war. He called for the Indians to "stand to their arms" rather than "be trampled as the serfs of Georgia."[9]

Making Money

The Mint Act of 1792 established the U.S. Mint. Two pieces of land were purchased in Philadelphia, which was the young nation's capital at the time. The first building housed the smelting furnace that separated the metals found in ore. Months later, the original U.S. Mint was established in what became called the Ye Olde Mint building. This is where gold and silver coins were first made. From time to time, branch mints, such as one in Georgia, operated where large deposits of gold or silver had been discovered. Today, U.S. coins are no longer made out of silver and gold.

them out of the state. Eleven Indian families enrolled in the emigration program in 1828.

THE GEORGIA LOTTERY

In 1832, Georgia lawmakers authorized the Georgia Lottery. It was the sixth of seven land lotteries in the state. One by one, 40-acre (16-ha) plots of land, called gold districts, were given away in drawings. Between October 1832 and December 1833, gold-laden land that belonged to the Cherokee was parceled out to Georgia residents. The land was so rich in gold that the United States set up a branch mint at Dahlonega, Georgia, where gold was converted into coins.

Prospectors finding gold in Georgia

Supreme Court Chief Justice John Marshall

To the Supreme Court

etween 1830 and 1850, as many as 100,000 American Indians, most of whom lived between Michigan, Louisiana, and Florida, were forced to leave their homelands and relocate west of the Mississippi River. Many did not go willingly. The Cherokee fought in legal battles that reached the U.S. Supreme Court.

Principal Chief John Ross took his tribe's grievances against the state of Georgia to the highest court in the land. Ross hired attorney William Wirt, who filed the suit that became *Cherokee Nation v. Georgia* on December 27, 1830.

This was the first time a suit filed by American Indians reached the U.S. Supreme Court. The lawsuit claimed that Georgia did not have jurisdiction over the Cherokee, an independent nation. It asked the Court to cancel all Georgia laws concerning the Cherokee and their land.

Instead, the U.S. Supreme Court announced that the Cherokee people were a dependent nation under the authority of the state and that the U.S. Supreme Court had no jurisdiction over the case. The Court also declared all American Indian tribes to be dependent nations.

This was a heavy blow to the Cherokee and other tribes. In the early 1830s, the Choctaws, the Creeks, and the Chickasaws gave in. They agreed to leave their lands. However, most of the Cherokee still refused to obey Georgia laws.

Spreading the Word

Missionaries from many Christian denominations served the Cherokee people. One mission was the Sarepta Baptist Missionary Society of Georgia. The school and church, established in 1821, were located near Gainesville, Georgia. The school had an average of 20 students per year.

Circuit-riding Methodist missionaries were common among the Cherokee. These missionaries were responsible for the Methodist churches within a given area. They also determined when more churches were needed. As they traveled from one church to another, they preached along the way in villages, fields, courthouses, and even people's homes. Methodists converted more Cherokee to Christianity than all the other denominations combined.

By 1830, more than 1,000 Cherokee were members of the Methodist Church.

ANOTHER COURT CHALLENGE

At that time, whites living among the Cherokee were required by Georgia law to obtain licenses of residency and take an oath of loyalty to the state. Eleven missionaries serving the Cherokee refused to abide by this law, claiming the state had no authority over the Cherokee Nation. In 1831, the missionaries were arrested. Nine decided to obey the law and obtained licenses. They were released from jail. But the other two missionaries—Samuel Worcester and Elizur Butler—refused to comply. They were tried, convicted, and sentenced to four years of hard labor in a Georgia penitentiary.

Worcester and Butler hired Wirt to appeal their case to the U.S. Supreme Court. In *Worcester v. Georgia*, the decision favored the Cherokee Nation. In a complete turnabout from the 1830 case, Chief Justice John Marshall wrote, "The Cherokee nation, then, is a distinct community, occupying its own territory . . . in which the laws of Georgia can have no force."[1]

The Court also declared that the laws of Georgia violated treaties between the United States and the Cherokee. It added that the arrest and conviction of Worcester violated federal law and the authority of the president of the United States. Elias Boudinot, editor of the *Cherokee Phoenix*, wrote enthusiastically to his brother:

> *It is glorious news. The laws of the state are declared by the highest judicial tribunal in the country to be null & void. It is a great triumph on the part of the Cherokee.*[2]

But President Andrew Jackson did not support Cherokee sovereignty. The state of Georgia ignored the Supreme Court's ruling and refused to release either Worcester or Butler. President Jackson called on the Cherokee to relocate or to be ruled by Georgia law. The Cherokee's hopes that the federal government would help them were shattered. They had nowhere else to turn.

Imprisoned

Samuel Worcester and Elizur Butler remained in the Georgia penitentiary until January 1833. The new Georgia governor, Wilson Lumpkin, worked with the Georgia legislature to repeal the law that had convicted them. The men then accepted a pardon from the governor.

In 1832, as many as 600 Cherokee voluntarily moved to present-day Arkansas. But they wrote letters to those they left behind urging them not to come. The government had not provided the promised food and supplies for the trip, and many Cherokee had died along the way.

Another Treaty and Another Offer

On July 23, 1832, the Cherokee Council met at Red Clay, Tennessee. U.S. Representative Elisha Chester presented a treaty that would remove the Cherokee from their land and relocate them west of the Mississippi. He argued that leaving Georgia was better than living under a hostile state government.

The Cherokee Council refused to sign the treaty, but some thought the treaty was worth considering. This included John Ridge, Elias Boudinot, William Hicks, James Starr, William Shorey Coodey, John Walker Jr., William Rogers, and Andrew Ross (the chief's brother). They became known as the Treaty Party.

The Cherokee were divided. Most wanted to stay in the Southeast, but others wanted to relocate. Boudinot felt strongly that the Cherokee should move and resigned from his position as editor of the

Cherokee Phoenix in protest. He told Chief Ross that it was time to tell the truth—that it was dangerous to resist removal any longer.

That year, President Jackson offered the Cherokee approximately $3 million to move. Chief Ross refused. John Ridge criticized Ross's decision and suggested that the Cherokee negotiate a removal treaty with the United States. Ridge's idea, however, was not popular with most Cherokee.

The Treaty Party began private negotiations with Georgia and the United States. In 1834, members of the Treaty Party proposed a removal treaty. But the rest of the Cherokee Nation, now called the Nationalists, would not agree to it. Conflict among the Cherokee increased.

The Cherokee complained that the federal government had not lived up to the treaties. Leaders of the Cherokee tribe discouraged people from emigrating, but some feared the consequences of staying more.

In 1834, approximately 500 Cherokee left voluntarily on flatboats

Father of a Nation

Principal Chief John Ross's Cherokee name was Kooweskoowe, after a mythological bird. He has also been called the Father of the Cherokee Nation and the Cherokee Moses for leading his people out of their homeland to a new territory. Ross served as principal chief of the Cherokee Nation through 1866. He died on August 1, 1866, at the age of 75.

to go to Indian Territory. Traders along the way increased their prices on food and whiskey. An outbreak of measles spread disease and death throughout the boats. During the trip, 81 people died.

As many as 500 Cherokee met with U.S. government officials at New Echota, Georgia, the center of the Cherokee government, on December 29, 1835. Records vary, but approximately only 80 to 100 of those present were voting members of the tribe. The others were women and children.

Stripped of Freedom

The Treaty of New Echota was signed on December 29, 1835. It signaled the relocation of the Cherokee Nation to lands west of the Mississippi River by May 1838.

In part, the treaty read:

The Cherokee nation hereby cede, relinquish, and convey to the United States all the lands owned, claimed, or possessed by them east of the Mississippi river, and hereby release all their claims upon the United States for [property] of every kind for and in consideration of the sum of five millions of dollars to be expended, paid, and invested in the manner stipulated and agreed upon in the following articles.[3]

In his letter to the U.S. Senate and House of Representatives, Chief Ross made a passionate plea for the Cherokee Nation:

We are stripped of every attribute of freedom. . . . Our property may be plundered before our eyes; violence may be committed on our persons; even our lives may be taken away, and there is none to regard our complaints. . . . We are deprived of membership in the human family! We have neither land nor home, nor resting place that can be called our own.[4]

The treaty was not revoked.

Ross and the rest of the Cherokee Nation refused to attend. That day, approximately 20 Cherokee signed the Treaty of New Echota, agreeing to a total removal of the Cherokee Nation from land east of the Mississippi River. In return, the Cherokee Nation was to receive $5 million.

The fate of 16,000 Cherokee was sealed by the signatures of 20 members of the tribe. The treaty set May 23, 1838, as a deadline for all Cherokee to relocate. Chief Ross told his tribe to ignore the treaty.

In a September 28, 1836, letter to Congress, Ross urged the government to repeal the treaty. His letter was ignored, and groups of Cherokee began migrating westward. Early in 1837, members of the Treaty Party volunteered to move to the West. The Cherokee who had signed away their land were equipped with supplies by the U.S. government. With their families, livestock, and slaves, they boarded boats for the trip west.

From 1836 to 1838, approximately 2,000 Cherokee voluntarily moved to present-day eastern Oklahoma. Other tribes in the Southeast had already agreed to similar treaties and headed west. But most of the Cherokee stood behind John Ross and refused to leave their homeland. It would take the U.S. military to round them up and force them to leave.

A Proclamation

Newly appointed General Winfield Scott set up U.S. Army headquarters in New Echota. On May 10, 1838, he issued a proclamation to the Cherokee people:

> *Cherokees! The President of the United States has sent me with a powerful army, to cause you, in obedience to the treaty of 1835 [Treaty of New Echota], to join that part of your people . . . on the other side of the Mississippi. . . . I am an old warrior, and have been present at many a scene of slaughter, but spare me, I beseech you, the horror of witnessing the destruction of the Cherokees. . . . Do not . . . wait for the close approach of the troops; but make such preparations for emigration as you can.*[5]

The Cherokee would leave, but they would not go willingly.

THE CASE

OF

THE CHEROKEE NATION

against

THF STATE OF GEORGIA:

ARGUED AND DETERMINED AT

THE SUPREME COURT OF THE UNITED STATES,

JANUARY TERM 1831.

WITH

AN APPENDIX,

Containing the Opinion of Chancellor Kent on the Case ; the Treaties between
the United States and the Cherokee Indians ; tne Act of Congress of
1802, entitled ' An Act to regulate intercourse with the Indian
tribes, &c.'; and the Laws of Georgia relative to the
country occupied by the Cherokee Indians,
within the boundary of that State.

BY RICHARD PETERS,

COUNSELLOR AT LAW.

A 1831 Supreme Court record of Cherokee Nation v. State of Georgia

President Martin Van Buren

Time Is Up

In 1836, the United States elected a new president, and Georgia elected a new governor. But nothing had changed for the Cherokee Nation. President Martin Van Buren and Georgia's governor upheld Cherokee removal.

The Treaty of New Echota had set May 23, 1838, as the deadline for Cherokee removal. On that date, Chief Ross was in Washington DC trying to convince the government not to follow through. But on May 26, General Winfield Scott ordered 7,000 troops to prepare for Indian removal. Their first task was to build stockades at locations throughout the Cherokee Nation. The stockades would serve as prisons for Cherokee as they waited to be escorted out of the state. By summer, the stockades were completed. Some Indians voluntarily made their way to the prisons to await emigration.

No Choice

Lieutenant John Phelps was with his regiment in the mountains when some of the Cherokee gave themselves up. The Cherokee had no choice but to leave their home and go to new, uncertain surroundings. What Phelps saw affected him deeply. He wrote in his journal, "They had never given their consent. They did not know what to expect."[1] The day Phelps left, some white Americans arrived to lay claim to Cherokee property. A few paid a very small amount for goods the Cherokee had left behind. Others just took what they wanted.

Cherokee who did not willingly leave were forced from their houses and land by soldiers armed with rifles and bayonets. Troops spread out to seize every Cherokee man, woman, and child by surprise. Cherokee families were not prepared for the arrival of armed soldiers.

With no opportunity to grab a precious memento or necessary belongings, the Cherokee were herded from their homes and led to the nearest stockade. Soldiers and looters followed in the wake of the tragedy to plunder anything of value. They set many homes ablaze. James Mooney, a white man who lived among the Cherokee, recalled, "Systematic hunts were made by the same men for Indian graves, to rob them of the silver pendants and other valuables deposited with the dead."[2]

A June entry in the journal of a missionary in Tennessee read:

> [W]e were disturbed by the arrival of a company of soldiers with 200 poor prisoners, Indians, soaked through by the rain, whom they drove through the Chickamauga River before them like cattle. . . . It was pitiful to see the poor folks, many old and sick, many little children, many with heavy packs on their backs, and all utterly exhausted.

In the confusion some had left behind their children, who chanced not to be at home; other children had run away from their parents in terror. [3]

Few Cherokee resisted; Chief Ross had advised them not to resort to violence. And the army had already taken away most of their weapons. General Scott ordered his soldiers to treat the Indians with "every possible kindness" [4] to avoid uprisings or war. But his orders were not always obeyed. Soldiers in the state militia were especially brutal.

Scott further explained that if Cherokee hid in the mountains or forests, they "must be pursued and invited to surrender, but not fired upon unless they should make a stand to resist." [5] Some Cherokee did manage to escape and hid in mountain caves or homes of sympathetic whites. When fleeing Cherokee were captured, Scott's orders were again ignored. They were either killed on the spot or brought

Hopelessness

On June 21, 1838, Lieutenant Phelps wrote in his journal. He described the last worship service the Cherokee conducted on their land. One of them prayed, acknowledging that this was the last time they would meet together in their place of worship. Phelps wrote of their overall feeling of hopelessness:

"They had left their homes, their neat gardens and fields, their stock and poultry, as tho' they were going to church, and even thus were they to set out upon their journey for the land from which they expected nothing but sickness and death." [6]

to the stockades. Firing squads were prepared to dole out swift and permanent punishment.

HARSH IMPRISONMENT

Eventually the stockades overflowed with frightened Cherokee of all ages. Life in the stockades was harsh and inhumane. Each stockade was built with split logs sharpened to a point at the top and lined up to form walls about 16 feet (5 m) high and surrounded an area approximately 200 by 500 feet (61 by 152 m).

The people had no way to cook food. The dirty drinking water kept them alive, but it also made

---

The Day the Soldiers Came

James Mooney, a white man who lived among the Cherokee, described this tragic scene:

Families at dinner were startled by the sudden gleam of bayonets in the doorway and rose up to be driven with blows and oaths along the weary miles of trail that led to the stockade. Men were seized in their fields or going along the road, women were taken from their wheels and children from their play.[7]

Ooloocha, a widowed Cherokee, remembered the day the soldiers came:

The soldiers came and took us from home. They first surrounded our house and they took the mare while we were at work in the fields and they drove us out of doors and did not permit us to take anything with us . . . would not permit any of us to enter the house to get any clothing but drove us off to a fort that was built at New Echota.[8]

them sick. There was no privacy. They slept on the ground, sometimes in mud. With no roof, they were subject to both rain and burning sun. Unbearable heat during one summer made survival a daily challenge. Sickness, disease, and exposure robbed hundreds of people of their lives, especially the very old and very young.

Daily food rations consisted of flour and salt pork. This was quite a contrast to an Indian's regular diet of meat, vegetables, and fruit. The pork they were given was not always cooked and sometimes was eaten raw. This led to a variety of illnesses. When traders added whiskey to the diet of the Indians, drunkenness led to shouting and fighting. In turn, this sometimes led to injuries, deaths, and abuse.

Approximately 16,000 Cherokee suffered in the stockades. Dysentery, fever, whooping cough, and measles took many lives. Hope quickly turned to despair. Missionaries in the stockades who had lived and worked with the Cherokee for decades refused to leave during this time of trial. They continued their religious work in the stockades. At Fort Butler, North Carolina, church services were conducted, and permission was given to baptize ten converts in a nearby river.

Stockade

The only remaining trace of the Cherokee stockades is a log blockhouse at Fort Marr in Old Fort, Tennessee. After the 1838 Indian removal, the building was sold to a private party and used as a chicken house.

Eventually, the owner donated it to Polk County, Tennessee. In 1965, the building was moved 15 miles (24 km) north to make room for U.S. Highway 411. This last remnant of a Cherokee stockade is open to visitors.

One Baptist missionary, Evan Jones, witnessed the people he had served being taken prisoner. He watched as "the tears gushed from their eyes."[9] The Cherokee would soon begin their journey west. Their march of exile would come to be known as *Nunna dual Tsuny*—"the trail where we cried."

General Winfield Scott

This flatboat is similar to those used to transport the Cherokee to the West.

THE TRAIL OF TEARS

On June 6, 1838, six flatboats rocked on the Tennessee River at Ross's Landing, now Chattanooga, Tennessee. As many as 3,000 Cherokee were taken from the stockades, divided into smaller groups, and crowded onto the boats.

Nearby, a steamship waited for orders to tow the boats downstream.

Daniel Butrick wrote in his journal that the people were "literally crammed into the boat . . . [that] was so filled that the timbers began to crack and give way, and the boat itself was on the point of sinking."[1] The unusual fleet slowly made its way down the Tennessee River. Treacherous rapids were ahead, and two flatboats at a time were maneuvered through the fast-moving water. Several days and four rivers later, the exiles were deposited at Sallisaw Creek in eastern Oklahoma.

Back in the stockades, the rest of the Cherokee awaited their removal and westward journey. By now, hundreds of them were sick and dying from the filthy conditions in their makeshift prisons. The death toll among babies and the elderly was especially high. They had little chance to survive in their disease-infested surroundings. Butrick wrote in his journal that this was "a most expensive and painful way of putting these poor people to death."[2]

A Second Migration

In July, Chief Ross returned to Georgia from Washington DC. Cherokee homes and crops had

Cherokee Chief John Ross

been burned and looted. Stray cattle and sheep now roamed the land. New Echota, once the Cherokee capital, was now an army camp for General Winfield Scott's troops. As awful as these sights were, Ross was particularly troubled by the horrifying conditions in the stockades. He appointed three people to regularly inspect the camps and report back on what the prisoners needed. Ross also banned alcohol in the stockades.

After hearing about the first migration during the heat and drought of summer, Ross asked General Scott to postpone subsequent trips until September. He also asked that the Cherokee be able to organize the migration themselves using government transportation and funds. Scott granted his request and placed the Cherokee Council in charge of relocation. Ross was given a new title—Superintendent of Cherokee Removal and Subsistence.

The remaining Cherokee prepared to leave their beloved land. In September, Ross and his committee of five other Cherokee divided the prisoners into 13 groups of approximately 1,000 each. Their plan was to travel by land since the drought had left river levels low.

Ancient Land

On August 1, 1838, the Cherokee signed their last resolution before leaving their land. As a nation, they declared, "The title of the Cherokee people to their lands is the most ancient, pure, and absolute, known to man; its date is beyond the reach of human record; its validity confirmed and illustrated by possession and enjoyment, [before] all pretense of claim by any other portion of the human race."[3]

The document also announced that "the original title and ownership of said lands still rest in the Cherokee Nation, unimpaired and absolute."[4]

Ross appointed a leader for each group. They included Jesse Bushyhead, Elijah Hicks, George Hicks, and others. U.S. soldiers who went along were to be observers only. The U.S. government would provide food and other supplies. The government also agreed to pay for the personal property the Cherokee were leaving behind—houses, furniture, cattle, and horses. The wealthy and the poor alike submitted bills for their belongings to the United States. But few people were ever paid.

Former President Andrew Jackson was furious that Ross was in charge of the removal. Despite Jackson's complaints, Ross remained in charge. With the help of General Scott, Ross brought in 645 wagons, 5,000 horses, and numerous oxen for the lengthy trip.

On October 1, 1838, the first group of Cherokee, numbering 1,103, gathered at Rattlesnake Springs, Tennessee, to begin their trek of 800 miles (1,287 km). Other Cherokee groups would follow in October and November. Most of the groups would take the northern route and board a ferry to cross the Mississippi River to Cape Girardeau, Missouri. Then they would travel south to Fayetteville, Arkansas, and on to eastern Oklahoma.

HARDSHIP AND DANGER

When the first of Ross's groups was ready to leave, he stood on one of the wagons and prayed. To the west, a dark spiral cloud appeared, and thunder rumbled. His nephew, William Shorey Coodey, and other Cherokee regarded the cloud and thunder as an omen.

A bugle sounded, and the procession started moving. The people were extremely weak from living in the stockades. But still most of them walked, despite the lack of shoes and clothing. They carried their few possessions or babies in their arms or on their backs. The very sick and the elderly rode in wagons. The wagons also carried the meager food and supplies for the people and the horses.

The journey ahead was expected to take from three to six months. Hardships and dangers lurked along the trail. When the Cherokee passed through private land, some landowners made them pay a toll, charging outlandish prices for each wagon and horse. When the Cherokee had to buy supplies, white residents often doubled or tripled their prices. They

Treaty Supporters

About 700 Cherokee—supporters of the Treaty Party—refused to travel under Ross's leadership. They formed their own group. By their request, they made the trip under the supervision of a U.S. Army officer.

demanded fees for burying Cherokee who died along the trail. The cost of a ferry went up for the Indians.

Every 10 to 15 miles (16 to 24 km), a good journey for a day, a campsite had been prepared in advance. Ideally, each site had wood fires, drinking water, and fields where horses could graze. But water was scarce due to the drought, and some wells had dried up. Sometimes groups did not make it to the camp by the end of the day and slept wherever they stopped.

One full-blooded Cherokee wrote about the journey:

Long time we travel on way to new land. People feel bad when they leave Old Nation. Womens cry and make sad wails. Children cry and many men cry, and

---

A Trail of Hardships

Conditions along the trail were harsh. Bad weather, disease, danger, exhaustion, and death haunted the Cherokee along the way. They often pitched their tents in deep snow, pouring rain, or gusting winds. Winter blizzards and brutal cold stranded groups at least a month at the southern tip of Illinois before they could cross the icy Mississippi River.

Drinking water was in short supply and sometimes contaminated. Chief White Path was just one of the many who died from drinking tainted water. Measles, whooping cough, dysentery, pneumonia, and tuberculosis were rampant. Cherokee died every day and were buried in shallow, makeshift graves beside the trail. Babies were born wherever a mother could find a spot to deliver. But most newborns did not survive. Many of the tears of this trail were for loved ones who would never make it to the new land.

---

all look sad like when friends die, but they say nothing and just put heads down and keep on go towards West. Many days pass and people die very much.[5]

The next day, that man's father fell in the snow and died. He was buried next to the trail. Days later, his mother died, followed by his five brothers and sisters—who died one day after the other. "Looks like maybe all be dead before we get to new Indian country," the Cherokee man lamented.[6] People were sick and dying. It was truly a time of weeping and wailing for the Cherokee people.

The final group of approximately 230 Cherokee left the stockades in December 1838. They journeyed on flatboats since water levels on the rivers had risen. These people were either too old or too ill to have made any of the previous journeys by land. John Ross, who had seen the other groups off, now traveled with this last group. He would not escape

Historic Trail

The Trail of Tears, the path the Cherokee took to the West, is now one of 19 national historic trails in the U.S. National Trail System. The historic trail goes through parts of nine states. It includes about 2,200 miles (3,540 km) of land and water routes.

Only a few groups of Cherokee were relocated using water routes. The majority of the Cherokee made their way to present-day Oklahoma by land routes.

the suffering that so many before him had already endured. On February 1, 1839, just before landing at Little Rock, Arkansas, his wife, Quatie, died. Ross buried his wife in a shallow grave chopped into the frozen ground.

Elizur Butler was also with this group. The missionary who had spent time in a Georgia prison for the cause of the Cherokee now mourned for the dying on the Trail of Tears.

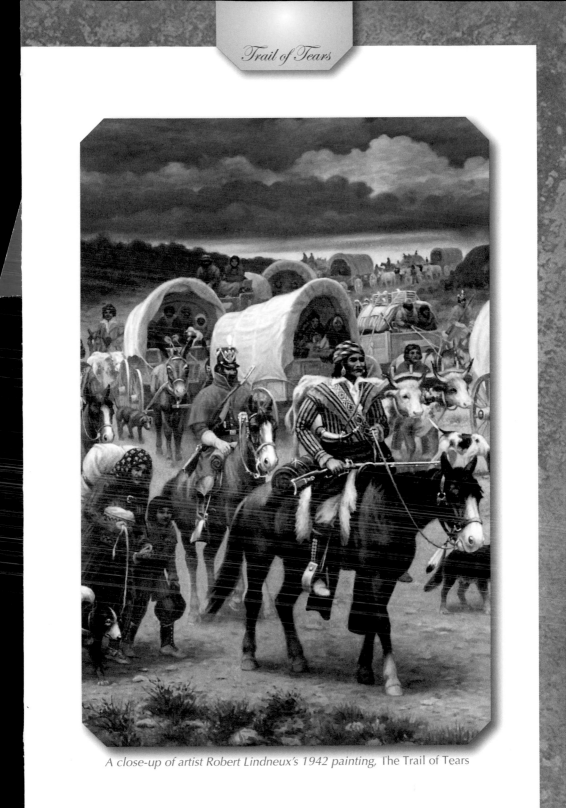

A close-up of artist Robert Lindneux's 1942 painting, The Trail of Tears

Chapter 9

Cherokee Chief John Ridge

New Land,
New Government

Thousands of Cherokee plodded through snowy trails, crossed icy rivers, and buried their dead. Even before the Cherokee had arrived at their new land, President Martin Van Buren celebrated the success of Indian removal. In his

December 3, 1838, State of the Union address, he remarked, "they have emigrated without any apparent reluctance." He went on to say that the government's "dealings with the Indian tribes have been just and friendly throughout."[1]

In February and March of 1839, the Cherokee people finally arrived in an area designated as Indian Territory. Approximately 4,000 people—25 percent of the tribe—had died along the Trail of Tears.

According to the Treaty of New Echota, the United States promised to provide food and supplies to the Cherokee for one year. But suppliers in the West wanted high prices for their meat, grain, and corn. When the government refused to pay those prices, the Cherokee sometimes did not receive their rations. And with tents for houses and no proper storage facilities, the food they did get often spoiled. At first, the exiles depended on these rations of rotten meat and bug-infested flour and cereal to survive. But with determination, they began to establish a new life and rebuild the Cherokee Nation.

SHARING LAND BUT NOT LOYALTIES

Since the Cherokee came to their new land with few supplies, utensils, or tools, they turned to traditional skills to survive. They made pots and dishes of clay and moccasins for their feet from deerskin. They erected houses and planted fields.

But soon the 14,000 Cherokee led by Chief Ross—the National Party—realized that the best land had already been taken. It was inhabited by Cherokee who had voluntarily come before them. These Cherokee comprised two groups. Approximately 3,000 were Old Settlers, Cherokee who migrated west prior to 1838. They had already established their society with their

Indian Territory

Indian Territory was land set aside by the United States for relocation of American Indians. The Indian Intercourse Act of 1834 set borders for the territory. These stretched from the Red River on the north border of Texas to the Missouri River along the northern border of Nebraska. The eastern border was the Mississippi River. The territory included present-day Oklahoma, Kansas, and Nebraska.

Portions of the land were designated for the Five Civilized Tribes: the Cherokee, the Choctaw, the Creek, the Chickasaw, and the Seminole. Each tribe set up its own government and towns such as Tulsa, Ardmore, Tahlequah, Tishomingo, and Muskogee. These towns have become some of the larger cities in the state of Oklahoma. Over time, the borders of Indian Territory diminished to what is now only the eastern half of Oklahoma.

In 1889, the United States opened up western Oklahoma to whites. In 1905, the people living in Indian Territory tried to be admitted to the Union as a state called Sequoyah. But Congress rejected the idea. In 1907, the state of Oklahoma was admitted to the Union. The borders of the state included Indian Territory, which then ceased to exist.

own government and laws. The other group included approximately 2,000 members and supporters of the Treaty Party.

Relations were still tense between these two groups. It would be a challenge for the members of the National Party and the Treaty Party to live together and share the same land.

Within a few months, conflicts arose over divided loyalties, land, and different governments. But the most burning conflict was between the National Party and the Treaty Party—traitors according to Ross's followers. They believed the Treaty Party had sold out the tribe by signing the Treaty of New Echota. As many as 150 men from the National Party met secretly to make a list of those in the Treaty Party who should be punished for selling tribal land.

On the morning of June 22, 1839, a group of Cherokee men attacked John Ridge, one of the men on the list. They dragged him from his bed and stabbed him to death while his wife and children looked on. Another group shot and killed John Ridge's father as he walked along an Arkansas road. At about that same time, a third group arrived at the home of Elias Boudinot. They said they had come to pick up medicine from the nearby mission.

But as Boudinot turned to get the medicine, one man stabbed him in the back, and another man split his head open with a tomahawk. All three victims had signed the Treaty of New Echota.

Other treaty signers were warned of the attacks and fled. Boudinot's brother, Stand Watie, promised revenge and plotted to kill Chief Ross. Several hundred armed Cherokee from the National Party surrounded Ross's house to protect him in case of such an attack.

Forming a New Government amid Ongoing Conflict

In June 1839, Chief Ross reminded the Cherokee that they were all a part of "the household of the Cherokee family and of one blood." He encouraged them to "rekindle their social fire" because "a House divided against itself cannot stand."[2]

On July 1, 1839, members of the National Party met and officially granted pardons to the men who had murdered John Ridge, Major Ridge, and Elias Boudinot. Eleven days later, the Old Settlers and the National Party signed a covenant, agreeing to unite and form one political body called the Cherokee Nation.

The two groups formed one new government and constitution similar to the National Party's previous structure. John Ross was elected principal chief, and David Vann of the Old Settlers was elected the assistant chief.

President Van Buren, however, refused to recognize the Cherokee Nation's new government. When Ross and other delegates visited Washington DC in 1840, Van Buren would not meet with them. The United States considered the Treaty Party the true Cherokee patriots.

In 1841, a new president took office. William Henry Harrison served just one month before he died of pneumonia. Vice President John Tyler became president. Tyler's administration established good relations with Ross's group of Cherokee. Tyler told Chief Ross in 1841, "You may assure your people that not justice merely shall be done them, but a liberal and generous policy will be adopted toward them."[3]

Sophia Sawyer

In 1823, Sophia Sawyer was a missionary to the Cherokee. During their forced relocation, Sawyer traveled with John Ridge and his family, who were part of the Treaty Party. After Ridge was murdered in Oklahoma, Sawyer fled with Ridge's wife, Sarah Bird Northrup Ridge, and 14 Cherokee girls to Fayetteville, Arkansas.

Sawyer founded the Fayetteville Female Seminary in Arkansas in 1839. The school provided education for Indian and white girls at a time when women received little instruction. Students boarded at the school or stayed with local families. At its peak, the school had 103 students and classes in music, French, literature, and embroidery.

Making Progress

In the early 1840s, the Cherokee established a public school system. In 1844, the tribal newspaper, the *Cherokee Advocate*, reported news about the Cherokee Nation as well as the United States.

Tahlequah, Oklahoma, the Cherokee capital, grew into a bustling city. The city streets were modernized, and housing was improved. The capital city was home to the Cherokee Supreme Court. Tahlequah was also the site of the Council House where Indian representatives met regularly.

Ross tried to negotiate a new treaty with the new administration but was unsuccessful. By the end of 1841, nearly three years after the tribe arrived at their new land, the Cherokee were living in poverty. They lacked proper tools and equipment to farm their crops; houses were sufficient but uncomfortable.

In the summer of 1842, the ongoing conflict between the National Party and the Treaty Party erupted once again. Members of the Treaty Party killed Cherokee they thought were behind the murders of their leaders in 1839. At the 1843 Cherokee Nation elections, people counting ballots were attacked, and the ballots were destroyed. Amid the chaos, John Ross won the election for principal chief. Violence, murders, and robberies persisted for years. The situation became so dire that members of the Treaty Party fled to Arkansas and demanded U.S. military protection.

Meanwhile, Ross tried to negotiate a new treaty with the United States. But in 1845, a new president, James Polk, set the Cherokee Nation back once again. Polk, who had no sympathy for the Cherokee, would not recognize Ross as the nation's chief.

The following year, Polk and Congress created the Treaty of 1846. It was signed by members of the National Party, the Treaty Party, and the Old Settlers. The treaty recognized that the differences that existed between the groups needed to be settled in order to restore peace. The parties hoped the treaty would bring unity to a divided tribe.

GROWTH AND TURMOIL

In 1849, the California Gold Rush was under way, and business was booming in Indian Territory. Gold prospectors stopped for supplies and food on their way to California. By October 1857, Ross was proudly reporting the progress to the Cherokee Council:

> Well cultivated farms, which have yielded abundant crops of grain, . . . well filled public schools, large and orderly assemblies, and quiet neighborhoods, which were seen in all the districts, showed marked improvement.[4]

By 1860, the Cherokee Nation had 21,000 members. Their community also included 4,000 African-American slaves. Horses, cattle, sheep, and land added to their wealth. In 30 public schools, classes were taught almost entirely by Cherokee teachers.

On April 12, 1861, the United States fell into turmoil. Northern and Southern states went to war against each other. For the next four years, the country would be embroiled in the American Civil War. The Cherokee Nation would again be divided politically. Some of the Cherokee, led by Stand Watie of the Treaty Party, supported the Southern Confederacy; others, under John Ross, initially took a strictly neutral position.

Ross found it difficult to stay neutral, however. In October 1861, in an attempt to maintain Cherokee unity, Ross joined the Treaty Party in its support of the South. The Confederate flag was raised over the capitol in Tahlequah, Oklahoma. In July 1862, Ross was captured by the North and taken as a prisoner of war. Stand Watie appointed himself principal chief of the Cherokee Nation.

The Civil War ended in defeat for the South in 1865. The Cherokee Nation, like the South, was left

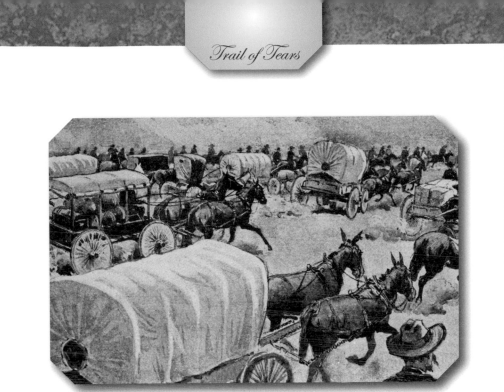

Pioneers rushed to obtain land that belonged to the Cherokee.

destitute. Released from prison, Ross moved back home. He assumed power of the nation and regained support of the federal government. During the next several years, the Cherokee worked hard to recover from the war and remain unified.

The Beginning of the End

A year after the war ended, in July 1866, the United States and the Cherokee Nation entered into yet another treaty—the Treaty of 1866. The Cherokee agreed to free their slaves and cede more land to

Tahlequah

Today, the city of Tahlequah, Oklahoma, is the seat of Cherokee County. It is also the capital of the Cherokee Nation and the United Keetoowah Band of Cherokee.

Some street signs and store signs are in English and Cherokee, using the syllabary created by Sequoyah in 1821. The city has a population of approximately 14,500 people. Approximately 33 percent of its citizens are American Indians.

the United States. They also granted a right-of-way through their land for the railroad, which would bring thousands of Americans to the West.

On August 1, 1866, at the age of 75, John Ross died in Washington DC. He had led the Cherokee Nation as principal chief for nearly 40 years. The Cherokee Nation brought the body of their chief back to Oklahoma.

From 1889 to 1895, the United States opened up land in Oklahoma to settlers. This allowed settlers from the United States and other countries to claim land in Oklahoma. In the 1893 Cherokee Strip Land Run, 6 million acres (2.4 million ha) were opened up to settlers. The United States paid the Cherokee $1 per acre (0.4 ha).

In 1907, Oklahoma became a state, and the Cherokee Nation vanished from U.S. maps. The Cherokee became part of the state of Oklahoma. It would be nearly 70 years before the Cherokee would again be an independent, sovereign nation.

Stand Watie supported the Confederacy in the Civil War.

President Roosevelt was given a feather bonnet from Cherokee Chief Jerry Blythe during his 1936 visit to a Cherokee Nation Indian Reservation.

THE CHEROKEE TODAY

After 1907, when Oklahoma became the forty-sixth state, the Cherokee Nation did not exist in the eyes of the United States. The Cherokee people were no longer allowed to have their own government or elect their own leaders.

U.S. presidents took charge of appointing tribal chiefs. However, the Cherokee still sought out and elected their own chiefs. Although elected chiefs were not recognized by the U.S. government, there were two exceptions.

In 1938, the Cherokee elected J. B. Milam as principal chief. As a sign of goodwill, President Franklin D. Roosevelt recognized the election in 1941. Chief Milam's goals were to rebuild the tribal government as well as preserve Cherokee property and historical items.

In 1949, the Cherokee again elected a chief—W. W. Keeler—and President Harry Truman honored and affirmed the election. A successful businessman, Keeler also served as Chief Executive Officer for Phillips Petroleum Company. In 1952, Keeler funded and created the Cherokee Foundation. This nonprofit organization obtained and provided funds to improve the welfare, health, and education of the Cherokee people.

Keeping History

Jesse Bartley (J. B.) Milam served as chief of the Cherokee Nation from 1938 through 1949. He was one thirty-second Cherokee. Milam was extremely interested in the history of the Cherokee people and accumulated one of the largest libraries in the state of Oklahoma. He eventually became a life member and then director of the Oklahoma Historical Society.

A New Cherokee Nation and New Leadership

In 1971, President Richard Nixon signed into law an act that allowed the Cherokee to again elect their own leaders. By democratic election, the Cherokee officially reelected Keeler as principal chief. This reestablished the Cherokee Nation in Oklahoma.

In 1975, Ross Swimmer was elected chief and served for ten years. In 1976, the Cherokee people ratified a new constitution. The United Keetoowan Band of Cherokee, a separate group with its own government, is also in the same Oklahoma location. Conflict arose between the two tribal nations. Each claimed to be the only legal Cherokee government in Oklahoma.

In 1984, Swimmer and the Cherokee Council traveled to Red Clay, Tennessee, for a meeting with the Eastern Band of Cherokee. There, the two Cherokee councils reaffirmed the bonds of their ancestral heritage. This historic event was the first joint council meeting

Bureau of Indian Affairs

The Bureau of Indian Affairs (BIA) was established in 1824. It is the oldest bureau in the U.S. Department of the Interior. According to its Web site, the BIA provides services to approximately 1.7 million American Indians, Indian tribes, and Alaska natives. It manages 52.7 million acres (21.3 million ha) of land that belongs to Indian tribes and individuals.

The mission of the Bureau of Indian Affairs is to "enhance the quality of life, to promote economic opportunity, and to carry out the responsibility to protect and improve the trust assets of American Indians, Indian tribes, and Alaska Natives."[1]

between the two tribes. It was also the first time the tribes had met since their ancestors were separated on the Trail of Tears 146 years before.

In 1985, President Ronald Reagan appointed Chief Swimmer as the assistant secretary of the U.S. Department of Interior for Indian Affairs. To take the position, Swimmer had to resign his position as principal chief of the Cherokee Nation. According to the Cherokee Constitution, when a chief can no longer serve out a term, the tribe's deputy chief takes over.

Wilma Mankiller

Wilma Pearl Mankiller, the first female chief of the Cherokee Nation, was born in Tahlequah, Oklahoma, on November 18, 1945. She was the sixth of 11 children born to Charley Mankiller, a full-blooded Cherokee, and Clara Irene Sitton, a white woman of Dutch-Irish heritage.

Wilma's family lived on 160 acres (65 ha), called Mankiller Flats. The U.S. government had given her grandfather the land when Oklahoma became a state in 1907. As part of a government plan to mainstream American Indians into larger cities, her family moved to San Francisco, California, when Wilma was ten years old.

In 1969, at the age of 24, Mankiller became involved in the American-Indian rights movement. That year, a group of American Indians, including Mankiller, occupied Alcatraz Island in San Francisco Bay to bring attention to American Indian rights. Her involvement eventually took her back to Oklahoma. She added Cherokee traditions to her lifestyle and went into full-time service for the Cherokee Nation. She began as an economic stimulus coordinator. Eventually, she became deputy chief and then principal chief of the Cherokee Nation. She served as chief of the Cherokee Nation for ten years.

A Comanche Indian led dances at the Cherokee National Holiday powwow in Tahlequah, Oklahoma, in August 1997.

Deputy Chief Wilma Mankiller was sworn in as principal chief of the Cherokee Nation on December 15, 1985, to fulfill his term. She was the first female to serve in this position. When that term was up in 1987, Mankiller was elected chief. She was reelected in 1991 and served until 1995, when health issues prevented her from running again. Wilma Mankiller was succeeded by Joe Byrd, who served as chief from 1995 to 1999.

In 1999, the Cherokee elected Chadwick "Corntassel" Smith as principal chief. His focus was to protect and expand the Cherokee Nation. Before becoming chief, Smith had been director of tribal planning, legal historian, prosecutor for the Cherokee Nation, director of justice, and adviser to the tribal tax commission.

A People of the Future

In 2005, the Cherokee Nation and the Eastern Band of Cherokee met at Chattanooga, Tennessee, on land that once belonged to the Cherokee. Michell Hicks, principal chief of the Eastern Band of Cherokee, called the spot "a Cherokee place." He went on to remind the people of the time when the Cherokee were one tribe. "This place remembers before we were divided," he said, "when we were one great nation—the Cherokee Nation."[2]

Controversy

Joe Byrd was principal chief of the Cherokee Nation from 1995 to 1999. These four years were filled with crises and controversy. After years of accusations and investigations, Byrd was indicted by the Cherokee Nation Justice Courts for obstruction of justice and misuse of funds in the spring of 1997.

In retaliation, on May 21, 1997, Byrd shut off power to the Cherokee Nation Justice Complex, fired judges, and boarded up the building. During the Cherokee National Holiday (over the Labor Day weekend) Oklahoma SWAT teams and helicopters from the Bureau of Indian Affairs patrolled Cherokee land. Byrd was called to Washington DC to meet with Attorney General Janet Reno and Secretary of the Interior Bruce Babbitt. On September 9, 1997, Byrd signed over control of the tribe's law enforcement system to the Bureau of Indian Affairs.

Smith stated, "We are not a people of the past. We are a people of the present, and for many centuries, we will be a people of the future."[3]

Under the leadership of Smith, the Cherokee Nation expanded into real estate as well as agricultural and corporate businesses. This includes Cherokee Nation Industries, which generates employment opportunities for Cherokee.

The Cherokee Nation Education Corporation is a not-for-profit corporation. It offers educational assistance for tribal members. It also is involved in revitalizing the language and culture of the Cherokee people.

The past, present, and future of the Cherokee will always be part of America's history. But one chapter of that story—the injustice and greed that forced the Cherokee to walk the Trail of Tears—can teach future generations that racism, pride, and greed nearly destroyed a nation.

Cherokee Nation Principal Chief Chad Smith spoke at the Cherokee
National Holiday in Tahlequah, Oklahoma, on September 4, 2004.

TIMELINE

1754–1763	1785	1787
The Cherokee fight for the British in the French and Indian War.	The United States and the Cherokee sign the Treaty of Hopewell.	The U.S. Constitution is written. It gives the president and Congress authority over Indian affairs and trade.

1821	1827	1828
Sequoyah develops a syllabary. The Cherokee learn to read and write their language.	The Cherokee develop a constitution modeled after the U.S. Constitution.	John Ross is elected principal chief of the Cherokee Nation.

1791	1802	1803
The Treaty of Holston is signed and gives conditions for "civilizing" the Cherokee.	In the Compact of 1802, President Jefferson promises to remove Indians from the state of Georgia.	The United States purchases land, known as the Louisiana Purchase, from France and reserves the land for Indian relocation.

1829	1830	1830
Gold is discovered in Georgia. The governor declares that all Cherokee land belongs to the state.	Congress passes the Indian Removal Act.	Chief John Ross files *Cherokee Nation v. Georgia* in the U.S. Supreme Court.

TIMELINE

1835	1839	1846
The Treaty of New Echota removes the Cherokee Nation from land east of the Mississippi River.	The Cherokee arrive in Indian Territory in present-day Arkansas and Oklahoma.	U.S. President Polk crafts the Treaty of 1846 to bring unity to the divided Cherokee tribe.

1907	1984
Oklahoma becomes a state; the Cherokee are absorbed into the state. The U.S. government appoints chiefs.	The Cherokee Nation meets with the Eastern Band of Cherokee for the first time since the Trail of Tears.

1861	1866	1889–1895
The American Civil War begins; some Cherokee support the South.	In the Treaty of 1866, Cherokee agree to free their slaves and cede more land to the United States.	The United States opens up Oklahoma land to settlers and stages land runs.

1985	2005
Wilma Mankiller becomes the first woman to serve as principal chief of the Cherokee Nation.	The Cherokee Nation and the Eastern Band of Cherokee meet where their ancestors began the Trail of Tears.

ESSENTIAL FACTS

DATE OF EVENT

1831–1839

PLACE OF EVENT

❖ New Echota, Georgia

❖ Red Clay, Tennessee

❖ Cherokee, North Carolina

❖ Tahlequah, Oklahoma

❖ Arkansas

KEY PLAYERS

❖ President Thomas Jefferson

❖ Chief John Ross

❖ President Andrew Jackson

❖ U.S. Supreme Court

❖ General Winfield Scott

HIGHLIGHTS OF EVENT

❖ The Cherokee signed the Treaty of Hopewell on November 28, 1785. It defined new Cherokee boundaries but was not honored by the states under the U.S. Articles of Confederation.

❖ In the Compact of 1802, President Jefferson promised to remove the Cherokee from the state of Georgia.

❖ With the Louisiana Purchase of 1803, Jefferson believed Indians could live more peacefully west of the Mississippi River.

- ✤ The 1830 Indian Removal Act allowed President Jackson to give unsettled land west of the Mississippi River to Indians in exchange for their land in existing states.

- ✤ In 1830, the U.S. Supreme Court declared that the Cherokee people were a dependent nation under the authority of the state.

- ✤ In 1834, approximately 500 Cherokee left voluntarily on flatboats to go to Indian Territory.

- ✤ On December 29, 1835, approximately 500 Cherokee men, women, and children met with U.S. government officials at New Echota, Georgia, the center of Cherokee government. Twenty Cherokee signed the Treaty of New Echota, agreeing to a total removal of the Cherokee Nation from land east of the Mississippi River. This affected 16,000 Cherokee.

- ✤ In the summer of 1838, as many as 15,000 Cherokee were moved into stockades prior to the emigration west.

- ✤ From September to December 1938, Chief John Ross was in charge of the migration.

- ✤ In February and March of 1839, the Cherokee people arrived in present-day Arkansas and Oklahoma. Approximately 4,000 people—25 percent of the tribe—had died along the Trail of Tears.

- ✤ Between 1830 and 1850, most American Indians—as many as 100,000 people—left their homelands between Michigan, Louisiana, and Florida and relocated west of the Mississippi River.

QUOTE

"We are now about to take our leave and kind farewell to our native land, the country that the great spirit gave our Fathers . . . it is with sorrow that we are forced by the authority of the white man to quit [leave] the scenes of our childhood . . . we bid a final farewell to it and all we hold dear."—*George Hicks, a Cherokee leader*

ADDITIONAL RESOURCES

SELECT BIBLIOGRAPHY

Carter, Samuel III. *Cherokee Sunset: A Nation Betrayed: A Narrative of Travail and Triumph, Persecution and Exile*. Garden City, NJ: Doubleday & Company, Inc., 1976.

Duncan, DeWitt Clinton. "The Story of the Cherokees." *Sequoyah Research Center: American Native Press Archives*. 12 Nov. 2008 <http://anpa. ualr.edu/digital_library/indianvoices/DunStor.htm>.

Ehle, John. *Trail of Tears: The Rise and Fall of the Cherokee Nation*. New York: Doubleday, 1988.

Golden, Randy. "The Trail of Tears." *Our Georgia History*. 12 Nov. 2008 <http://ourgeorgiahistory.com/indians/cherokee/trail_of_tears.html>.

"Indian Removal Act." *History Central*. 10 Dec. 2008 <http://www. historycentral.com/Indians/RemovalAct.html>.

"Oral History of the Cherokee." *Indian Country Diaries*. 19 Nov. 2008 <http://www.pbs.org/indiancountry/history/oral1.html>.

Rozema, Vicki, ed. *Voices From the Trail of Tears*. Winston-Salem, NC: John F. Blair, 2004.

FURTHER READING

Bealer, Alex W. *Only the Names Remain: The Cherokees and the Trail of Tears*. Boston: Little, Brown and Company, 1972.

Byers, Ann. *The Trail of Tears: A Primary Source History of the Forced Relocation of the Cherokee Nation*. New York: Rosen Publishing Group, 2003.

Conley, Robert J., and David Fitzgerald. *Cherokee*. Portland, OR: Graphic Arts Center Publishing Company, 2002.

Long, Cathryn J. *The Cherokee*. San Diego: Lucent Books, 2000.

Web Links

To learn more about the Trail of Tears, visit ABDO Publishing Company online at **www.abdopublishing.com**. Web sites about the Trail of Tears are featured on our Book Links page. These links are routinely monitored and updated to provide the most current information available.

Places to Visit

Cherokee Heritage Center
21192 South Keeler, Park Hill, Tahlequah, OK 74465
888-999-6007
www.cherokeeheritage.org
This center promotes and preserves the Cherokee culture. Features include tours of Cherokee villages, a Trail of Tears exhibit, and a museum.

Museum of the Cherokee Indian
589 Tsali Boulevard, Cherokee, NC 28719
828-497-3481
www.cherokeemuseum.org
This museum offers educational and interactive displays of the history of the Cherokee. It highlights the Eastern Band of Cherokee who remained in North Carolina.

Red Clay State Historic Park
1140 Red Clay Park, Cleveland, TN 37311
423-478-0339
www.state.tn.us/environment/parks/RedClay/features/historic.shtml
Red Clay was the seat of Cherokee government from 1832 until the forced removal of the Cherokee in 1838. This historical park is an interpretive site on the Trail of Tears.

GLOSSARY

alliance
A close association between two or more nations or groups working together.

ancestral
Passed down through several generations.

boomtown
An area that experiences swift economic or population growth.

convert
To persuade someone to adopt a certain religion or belief.

delegation
A group of persons officially appointed to represent others.

drought
A long period of low rainfall.

ferry
A boat for transporting passengers and vehicles across a body of water.

heralded
Signaled the approach of an event or a person.

holocaust
An event that causes a brutally extensive loss of life.

immemorial
Existing beyond memory or tradition.

imminent
About to occur.

indicted
Charged with a crime.

land lotteries
Random drawings in which plots of land were given away by the government in the early 1800s.

land run
> A race by Americans to claim plots of land in the former Indian Territory in present-day Oklahoma.

legacy
> Property or history handed down from generation to generation.

migrate
> To move from one place, country, or locality to another.

negotiate
> To work with others to come to an agreement.

prospector
> A person who explores an area for mineral deposits.

rations
> Fixed amount of food allotted to members of a group.

sovereign
> Self-governing, independent.

stockade
> An enclosure made of strong posts and used as a jail.

syllabary
> A list of symbols representing the sounds of vowels and consonants.

treaty
> A formal agreement between two or more nations or groups.

SOURCE NOTES

Chapter 1. Nunna dual Tsuny
1. William Bartram. *Travels, and Other Writings.* New York: Library of America, 1996. 386–387.
2. Wilma Mankiller and Michael Wallis. *Mankiller: A Chief and Her People.* New York: St. Martin's Griffin, 1993. 77.
3. National Park Service. "Cherokee Removal—The Trail Where They Cried." 17 Jan. 2009 <http://www.powersource.com/cocinc/history/trail.htm>.
4. Wilma Mankiller and Michael Wallis. *Mankiller: A Chief and Her People.* New York: St. Martin's Griffin, 1993. 48–49.
5. Ibid. 255.

Chapter 2. West Is Black, Black Is Death
None

Chapter 3. This Land Is Our Land
None

Chapter 4. A Greater Degree of Civilization
1. "Treaty of Holston, July 2, 1791." *Roots Web Ancestry.* 24 Nov. 2008 <http://www.rootsweb.ancestry.com/~itcherok/treaties/1791-holston.htm>.
2. "An Act to Regulate Trade and Intercourse With the Indian Tribes, and to Preserve Peace on the Frontiers." *TNGenWeb Project.* 10 Dec. 2008 <http://www.tngenweb.org/tnland/intruders/17960519.html>.

Chapter 5. Gold!
1. Theda Perdue and Michael D. Green. *The Cherokee Nation and the Trail of Tears.* New York: Penguin/Viking, 2007. 58.
2. Nancy Roberts. *The Gold Seekers: Gold, Ghosts and Legends from Carolina to California.* Columbia, SC: University of South Carolina Press, 1989. 100.
3. Theda Perdue and Michael D. Green. *The Cherokee Nation and the Trail of Tears.* New York: Penguin/Viking, 2007. 63.
4. Samuel Carter III. *Cherokee Sunset: A Nation Betrayed.* Garden City, NY: Doubleday & Company, Inc., 1976. 97.
5. Ann Byers. *The Trail of Tears: A Primary Source History of the Forced Relocation of the Cherokee Nation.* New York: Rosen Publishing Group, 2003. 19–21.

6. Ibid.

7. Ibid.

8. "Treaty With the Western Cherokee, 1828." Indian Affairs: Laws and Treaties. Vol. II, Treaties. 18 Dec. 2008 <http://digital. library.okstate.edu/KAPPLER/Vol2/treaties/che0288.htm>.

9. Samuel Carter III. *Cherokee Sunset: A Nation Betrayed*. Garden City, NY: Doubleday & Company, Inc., 1976. 90–91.

Chapter 6. To the Supreme Court

1. *Worcester* v. *Georgia*. 31 U.S. (6 Pet.) 515 (1832). 3 Dec. 2008 <http://homepages.law.asu.edu/~rclinto/ConLaw1/ WORCESTER.pdf>

2. Robert J. Conley. *The Cherokee Nation: A History*. Albuquerque, NM: University of New Mexico Press, 2005. 135.

3. "Treaty of New Echota, December 29, 1835." *Cherokee Nation, Indian Territory Research, RootsWeb Ancestry*. 3 Dec. 2008 <http://www. rootsweb.ancestry.com/~itcherok/treaties/1835 new-echota.htm>.

4. "Letter from Chief John Ross of the Cherokee, Georgia, 1836." *History Matters*. 3 Dec. 2008 <http://historymatters.gmu. edu/d/6598/>.

5. "Gen. Winfield Scott's Address to the Cherokee Nation (May 10, 1838)." *GeorgiaInfo*. Digital Library of Georgia. 3 Dec. 2008 <http://georgiainfo.galileo.usg.edu/scottadd.htm>.

Chapter 7. Time Is Up

1. Sarah H. Hill, ed. *The Diary of Lt. John Phelps. Journal of Cherokee Studies, XXI*. Museum of the Cherokee Indian, 2000. 25.

2. Samuel Carter III. *Cherokee Sunset: A Nation Betrayed*. Garden City, NY: Doubleday & Company, Inc., 1976. 233–234.

3. Ibid. 238.

4. "Gen. Winfield Scott's Order to U.S. Troops Assigned to the Cherokee Removal." *GeorgiaInfo*. 17 May 1838. 4 Dec. 2008 <http:// georgiainfo.galileo.usg.edu/scottord.htm>.

5. Ibid.

6. Sarah H. Hill, ed. *The Diary of Lt. John Phelps. Journal of Cherokee Studies, XXI*. Museum of the Cherokee Indian, 2000. 24.

7. Samuel Carter III. *Cherokee Sunset: A Nation Betrayed*. Garden City, NY: Doubleday & Company, Inc., 1976. 232.

SOURCE NOTES CONTINUED

8. Theda Perdue and Michael D. Green. *The Cherokee Nation and the Trail of Tears*. New York: Penguin/Viking, 2007. 123–124.
9. Theda Perdue and Michael D. Green. *The Cherokee Removal: A Brief History With Documents*. Boston: Bedford/St. Martin's, 2005. 174.

Chapter 8. The Trail of Tears
1. Theda Perdue and Michael D. Green. *The Cherokee Nation and the Trail of Tears*. New York: Penguin/Viking, 2007. 127.
2. Samuel Carter III. *Cherokee Sunset: A Nation Betrayed*. Garden City, NY: Doubleday & Company, Inc., 1976. 245.
3. "The Last Resolution of the Original Cherokee Nation." 1 Aug. 1838. Chattanooga InterTribal Association (CITA). 10 Dec. 2008 <http://cita.chattanooga.org/1838rsn.htm>.
4. Ibid.
5. Thurman Wilkins. *Cherokee Tragedy: The Ridge Family and the Decimation of a People*. University of Oklahoma Press, 1986. 327.
6. Ibid.

Chapter 9. New Land, New Government
1. "Martin Van Buren: State of the Union 1838." 3 Dec. 1838. *From Revolution to Reconstruction*. 10 Dec. 2008 <http://www.let.rug.nl/usa/P/mb8/speeches/mb_1838.htm>.
2. Theda Perdue and Michael D. Green. *The Cherokee Nation and the Trail of Tears*. New York: Penguin/Viking, 2007. 147.
3. Samuel Carter III. *Cherokee Sunset: A Nation Betrayed*. Garden City, NY: Doubleday & Company, Inc., 1976. 274.
4. Quoted in Grant Foreman. *The Five Civilized Tribes*. Norman, OK: University of Oklahoma Press. 1934. 415.

Chapter 10. The Cherokee Today
1. "Indian Affairs." Bureau of Indian Affairs. 24 Feb. 2009 <http://www.doi.gov/bia/index.html>.
2. Theda Perdue and Michael D. Green. *The Cherokee Nation and the Trail of Tears*. New York: Penguin/Viking, 2007. 163.
3. Ibid. 164.

INDEX

INDEX CONTINUED

ABOUT THE AUTHOR

Sue Vander Hook has been writing and editing books for more than 15 years. Although her writing career began with several nonfiction books for adults, her main focus is educational books for children and young adults. She especially enjoys writing about historical events and biographies of people who made a difference. Her published works also include a high school curriculum and several series on disease, technology, and sports. Vander Hook lives with her family in Minnesota.

PHOTO CREDITS